Funded by the Government of Australia
Property of the Government of PNG
Not for resale

Yauka Aluambo Liria

OXFORD UNIVERSITY PRESS

Oxford New York
Auckland Bangkok Buenos Aires Cape Town
Chennai Dar es Salaam Delhi Hong Kong
Istanbul Karachi Kolkata Kuala Lumpur
Madrid Melbourne Mexico City Mumbai
Nairobi São Paulo Shanghai Taipei
Tokyo Toronto

Reprinted 1998, 1999, 2000 (twice), 2003, 2015(D)

ISBN 0 19 554097 2

Edited by Kate Deutrom and Eliza Collins
Text and cover design by Kirstin Lowe
Illustrations by Jon Kombeng
Printed in Australia by Ligare Pty Ltd
Published by Oxford University Press,
Editorial office: PO Box 7979, Boroko NCD,
Papua New Guinea

Contents

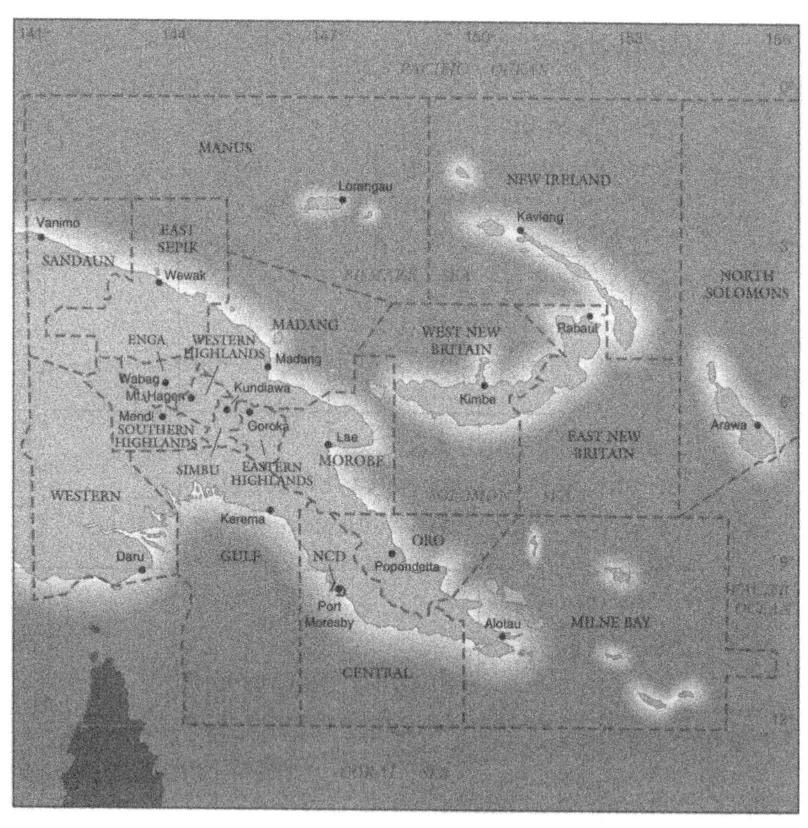

Papua New Guinea

Introduction

For thousands of years, our people have been responsible for their own survival. Our ancestors developed rich and diverse societies, with help from no one but themselves. Our unique cultures continue to enrich the lives of our people.

Today's young people, now find themselves *at the crossroads*. They have to make difficult decisions about which road to take. There are many obstacles along the way. We cannot always take the most direct route to reach our journey's end. We must be prepared to change direction and try another road. Above all, we should never give up.

The stories in this book are based on true life experiences of school leavers who did not give up. The author has interviewed school leavers from many parts of Papua New Guinea. It is hoped that the experiences highlighted in these stories will give hope to our young people as they continue with their life's journey.

There are no easy answers to solving the problems encountered by young people today. The purpose of this book is to get young people thinking about what they can do for themselves. They have to be able to make decisions for themselves, to feel confident about those decisions, while maintaining respect for the feelings of others.

Self reliance is needed just as much in today's society as it was in the past, so that our young people can assist in the process of nation building for the future needs of our diverse society.

The stories in this book are aimed at students in grades six to eight. They can be used as an integrated resource for subjects such as Guidance, Personal Development, English and Social Science. The questions at the end of each chapter encourage the students to reflect on the text, discuss what they have read, listen to the responses of others and suggest alternative strategies. The book should also be of interest to the general reader who wants to find out more about life in Papua New Guinea.

Disclaimer

To avoid any problems that may arise, all the names in the stories have been changed to 'nick names' chosen by the interviewees themselves. The stories were given to the author freely by citizens of Papua New Guinea, who feel strongly about the concept of self reliance and the need to help our young people tackle the challenges of living in a changing society.

1 I won't give up

Lina left Pangia High School in 1992 after completing grade 10. She comes from a remote village, some thirty kilometres southeast of Pangia High School.

After finishing grade ten, Lina did not get any offers to continue with her education. Lina made a secret decision to continue her education at home in the village, through CODE, the College of Distance Education. Her dream was to become a nurse.

This is a village girl's story about her determination to overcome the odds, to improve her education and further her career opportunities. It is the story of a girl's struggle in a remote village, in a culture where only boys were expected to make decisions and try new things. The girls were expected to get married, produce children, make plenty of gardens, raise lots of pigs and be good supporters of their husbands by being obedient wives.

This is Lina's story. It's a story of struggle and success.

At school, Lina did well in all subjects except English. However, all her job applications were unsuccessful because she had failed her English exam.

When she first returned home to the village she felt very depressed. She felt a failure, even though she had tried her best. She did not know how to react, or what to do, or how to explain her failure to her parents and other family members. She felt confused, embarrassed, and lonely.

She thought of running away to Mendi, or Nipa or Lae. But she didn't want to be a burden on the wantoks. She'd also heard lots of stories about what happened to young girls who went to town in search of work and she had the sense to realize that it wasn't a good idea for her.

She remembered what her mum had said when she first went to High School.

'You can always come home to live if you don't like school. We are your parents, we will understand. But, try hard and do your best. Never give up. If your plans don't work out the first time round, then give it another go. Don't accept defeat. Don't accept failure. Keep trying.' So she returned home and planned to tell her parents about her plans for the future.

Lina's mother was thrilled to have Lina home again. She was very proud that her daughter had completed grade 10 and didn't consider her a failure at all. She imagined that Lina would start to take an active role in village life and would soon find a husband for herself. In fact, Lina's mum had a few suggestions in mind!

During the Christmas holidays, Lina helped her mother with all the chores. She accompanied her mother everywhere. She told her mum,

'You know mum, I've never really helped you much before. Now, I am a big girl, I'm going to share all the work with you and learn how to be a good village girl. And maybe I'll have time to do some more studies, as well.'

Mum gave her a big hug and said,

'That's great, Lina, because I've got a lot of things to teach you. But I don't think there'll be time for doing studies. You've finished with that life now.'

Most of their time was spent with the pigs, in the coffee gardens or the food gardens. There was certainly a lot to do. Lina brought in a big bundle of firewood every afternoon and soon her mother's firewood pile was growing. Her mother was really pleased with her.

Lina was enjoying this time with her mum. She realised how hard her mother had worked in order to keep her at school. But at the same time, she couldn't help thinking about doing further studies. When she did the weeding she would often day-dream about how she could achieve her dream. She wanted to do further studies with CODE, the College of Distance Education.

Before leaving High School, she had had a serious talk with her class teacher about studying with CODE. Her teacher had said that it would be possible, as long as Lina had the money to pay for the registration fee. She only had to improve her English grade and then she could apply to do nursing training, something she had always wanted to do.

One day in January, Lina discussed this idea with her mother. Her mother listened carefully and then asked Lina,

'But who will help you when you have problems?'

'Well mum, every month I'll go to Mendi to see the CODE supervisors. They'll check my work and help me with any problems.' Her mother could not believe her ears. A girl walking some thirty kilometres to Pangia station and then another sixty kilometres by PMV to Mendi. It was too far away and where would she stay?

'Who will go with you. You couldn't possibly go alone.' She shook her head and said,

'Oh no, I'm sorry Lina but I think that it is going to be impossible. You could get raped on the road!'

'Oh come on mum, I'll be all right.'

'How do you know? How can you be sure? No, I'm

sorry Lina but the answer is no. It's best that you stay here and find a good husband and settle down with a family of your own.'

The two of them could not agree. They argued constantly and they were getting very upset. They both said things that they didn't really mean.

When Lina's mum shouted,

'Maybe you failed your English because you were chasing after boys,' Lina threatened to run away and never come back. They both broke down in tears. Mum sobbed,

'You know it's too risky to travel alone to Mendi every month. I'd go out of my mind with worry.'

However, Lina was determined she was going to do CODE. The argument eventually ended, but they did not reach any compromise. The issue was still unresolved.

Towards the end of January, Lina was becoming restless. She knew that she had to travel to Mendi to the CODE Centre so that she could enrol herself for the grade 10 English course. But her mother would not agree. Furthermore, her house had no lamp, chair or table.

By now, the whole village knew of Lina's wish to study with CODE. Most of the villagers didn't approve of Lina going to Mendi, especially her uncles. What was this girl up to? How could she study in a *kunai* house? Was she crazy? One of them asked,

'Taim bilong skul em stap we?'

Lina felt the whole world was against her. Her mother told her,

'My daughter, you see, the whole village does not like what you want to do. If I allow you to go and then you get raped on the road, they will put all the blame on me. Your father and uncles will never forgive me. Therefore, I am sorry but I still say no!'

Lina cried herself to sleep that night and the next day as well. Her eyes and face were swollen from so much crying.

That evening she left her mother's house. She planned to run away.

Lina's cousin-sisters came to her rescue. They knew how desperate she was to do her studies. They'd all felt the same despair when they could not continue on to High School. They put their money together and gave it to Lina. They wanted her to have a chance. They gave Lina fifty kina.

More tears filled Lina's eyes as she looked at her friends.

'You're the best cousin-sisters in the world. When I become a nurse I'll look after all of you and your babies when they get sick,' she said. All the girls were the same age as Lina. They had all completed grade six together, but Lina had been the only one to go to High School.

Now, they were learning how to be village mothers. Their village life teachers were their own mothers, their grandmothers and the wives of their uncles.

They learned how to be good wives, how to make bilums, make mats, weave umbrellas, sew grass skirts, cook food, grow food in the gardens, fish in the rivers, collect firewood, give birth to babies, and look after children. They also learned about looking after pigs so that the pigs could mature quickly. Furthermore, the older women taught them about their general behaviour in public, what to say and what not to say, how to walk or when to talk to somebody. Everything that you would find in Wiru village life was taught to them. And the girls had to learn quickly because they had husbands and children to look after.

Over the Christmas period, Lina's mother had started teaching her about village life. She had learned quite a lot and she had enjoyed these lessons in life. But Lina had a burning ambition to become a nurse. She would then come back to the village and put her nursing skills to good use by helping her village people.

But first, she had to pass her grade 10 English. And the only way to do that, was to enrol in the CODE course in Mendi. If she failed to improve her English grade at CODE, then she was prepared to settle down in the village and get married.

She explained her plan to the girls. They were all happy to help her. It was their custom to help each other in times of need. It was also their custom to share their wealth with each other. They knew that Lina would help them sometime in the future. That's how life is in the village.

So that's how Lina got her fifty kina. During the first week of February, she left for Mendi. She asked a cousin-brother to escort her to Pangia. Then, in the afternoon, she farewelled her cousin, took a PMV and went to Mendi. She found her wantok's house and asked them if she could stay there and do her CODE. They said she could stay until she got herself registered for her CODE course, but then she would have to return home.

Lina was worried about how her mother would react when she finally went home.

'When I return home I think mum and dad will support me in my studies,' she told herself. 'They'll realise how determined I am.'

So that is what she did. She returned with the CODE material, a dictionary and some writing material. Her cousin received Lina's travel arrangements over the

NBC's *toksave* program, and was there to meet her at Pangia to escort her on the long walk home.

Her mother was happy Lina had returned safely. Before Lina could say a word, her mother announced, 'Lina, you can do your correspondence course here. Come inside the house and see what we have prepared for you.'

There, in the corner of the house were a chair and table made from bush materials that her cousin-brothers had made especially for her. Her dad had smoothed out a tin-fish cardboard carton and put it on top of the table, to make a smooth surface so Lina could do her writing. There was also a new hurricane lamp and two bottles of kerosene.

'Oh thanks, mum and dad,' cried Lina as the tears ran down her face. Her mum gave her a big hug and said,

'Well, what do you say? Don't stand there crying. Why don't you try sitting on the chair? Let's see if it's big enough for you.'

Lina moved over and sat down. The table was perfect. The chair was too high but that was a minor problem. The legs could be shortened easily. Lina was so happy she cried with joy.

That night before going to bed, her mother explained what had happened. When Lina ran away, there was a big debate within the clan. Some agreed that Lina should be allowed to upgrade her English during the year. If that did not work out, then she should think about getting married. Others argued that she had wasted her time during school days, looking for boys instead of studying and now was not the time for school. She should therefore forget about CODE and get married. However, after a long debate, they finally agreed that they would give her another chance because she was showing such a strong determination to continue her studies.

None of them wanted her to run away and get into trouble. So, Lina's cousin-brothers were given the job of constructing Lina's CODE study table and chair. That job was done in three days.

Thus, Lina was ready to begin her CODE lessons by the middle of February. She had the support of her parents, other members of the clan and the other girls in the clan.

Before Lina got started, she recalled the advice of her high school class teacher.

'Always list down the time available to you for any job. Then, list down all the jobs or things that must be done over this time period. Finally, using these two lists, prepare a good, realistic programme or timetable for the week. It should cover Monday to Sunday. It should begin at 7.00 a.m. and finish at 8.00 p.m.

'Furthermore, make sure you are realistic about your timetable so that it can be followed easily. If you have difficulty following it or if you are making changes each week, it means you are not realistic in your programming.

'Also, talk to parents, grannies and girlfriends to make sure you include the jobs they want you to do each week, for example, collecting firewood; fetching water for cooking and drinking; weeding new gardens; clearing and digging new gardens and making ropes for bilums. Also think about the activities you may want to do with the other girls, for example, playing basketball or going to the local market together on Saturdays. Also include a full day or afternoon as a free period so you can do things that you have not programmed for.

'But always remember that since you are doing CODE, which is the same as doing school work, you must think and live like a student.

'Give priority to your main aim or objective. If your main objective for a year is to do CODE, then 70-80 per cent of your time, energy, thinking and resources must be directed towards achieving that aim. Other things and plans in your life can wait. Therefore, you must not set too many objectives for the year. Be realistic in your planning. Set only one objective each year, that you are confident you can achieve and go for it.

'Finally, after taking careful note of this advice, prepare your timetable. Try it out for two to three weeks. If it doesn't work out to your satisfaction then make changes to your timetable and you should be all right.

'If you follow this advice, it will help you to be successful. Remember: you must strictly follow your timetable if you want to succeed. If not you will certainly fail!'

Lina took this advice seriously and prepared her timetable. After two weeks of trying it out, she carefully made the necessary changes. She also promised herself to strictly follow her timetable.

By the middle of June, she had successfully completed half of the CODE units for the grade 10 English course. So far, her grades were average. If she continued with the same level of self-discipline, concentration and pure hard work, she knew, she would pass with a good grade.

So far her progress was good. Her parents gave her full support. Also, the village girls gave lots of support and encouragement. They too, were happy with Lina's progress and they were confident that she was going to finish with a good grade by November. They wanted her to become a nurse and come back to the village to help look after all of them, especially the babies. Consequently, their encouragement and support were strong.

Studying in a village environment was far more difficult than in a school environment. Lina had to be twice as determined to succeed. Here are some of the problems she faced.

The first problem was with village life in general. There was always something happening and lots of things to be done.

Pigs were whining for food. Children were screaming for mother's milk. Kids were laughing wildly whilst playing hide-and-seek. However, by nine o'clock in the morning, the village was very quiet, just like a cemetery. Everyone departed to go to the gardens, the bush, the creeks or the river. Then, she felt alone, sometimes too alone. And there was no one to ask for help when she got stuck on a problem. She was the only one doing school work.

Sometimes it was difficult to keep going. But she reminded herself that she was going through all this because she did not work hard enough at school. But she knew that if she kept going she would succeed. Everybody has their bad days and she must just get through it as best as she could.

Another big problem was getting to Mendi to hand in her completed units and collect new units. It was thirty kilometres to Pangia. The bush track went over big creeks, mountains, steep hills and jungles. Also, the track was muddy and rough. It was very tiring to walk this long distance.

Sometimes, Lina had to travel to Mendi twice a month to seek advice on difficult units and questions. Furthermore, the rascal activity in the area had increased and this presented many risks when walking to Pangia. However, she was usually escorted by her cousin-brothers.

Sometimes, the bigger boys got fed up of going and tried to send smaller kids instead! That was very frightening for her because rascals could easily scare off the younger boys and harm her. However, luckily for her, the clan members realised what was happening and made sure that the older boys always escorted her.

She also did her own deals with the older boys. If they agreed to escort her to and fro, for every month they did, she agreed to pay them some money when she started working. She told them they would have to wait a long time for this to happen but she would keep her promise to them. This made the boys feel a bit guilty and they always said they would do it for nothing. Thus, after the first few months, she faced no problems. Out of the three boys, at least two were always there to do the job they agreed on. On her part, she knew she had a promise to honour later.

Another major problem was getting help with difficult questions, exercises and readings. She needed to get help from someone living close by. Pangia High School and Mendi CODE centre were too far away. However, there was a community school about five kilometres from the village.

One day, she visited the school with her dad. They explained their problem to the Headmaster. They offered local food from their garden to be delivered once every week, as payment. The Headmaster said he was too busy to help, but he found a senior teacher who agreed to help.

Lina visited the senior teacher once each week for assistance and guidance. He was a great help to Lina and he made all the difference to her studies. When Lina completed her course in November, her daddy gave a medium-sized pig to the teacher. That was his way of saying thank you for helping his daughter.

Lina successfully finished her course in November. She received a C grade and was accepted into Goroka nursing college for a three year training course.

Lina's determination and hard work have paid off. She now has a bright future ahead of her. And also, she is more confident in herself because she succeeded the hard way.

Things to do

1. List the advantages and disadvantages of doing a correspondence course if you live in the village.
2. List the advantages and disadvantages of doing a correspondence course if you live in the town.
3. In groups, find out all you can about CODE in your area. Write a letter to CODE asking for information about courses.
4. Plan a weekly programme you would follow if you were doing a correspondence course while living in the village. Justify and explain your programme to your classmates.
5. When students want to continue their studies at home, they may encounter problems from relatives. In groups, act out this situation and show the conflict between the family and clan members and the debate that takes place between the family members and others in the village.

2 Never miss a chance

At just twelve years old Martin's life fell apart, or so he thought. When the announcement was made about which students had made it to grade seven, his name was not on the list. This is the story of a grade six school drop-out. Martin always hated that name. He didn't want to drop-out of school in the first place. He loved school and he had lots of friends. But he didn't get a place in High School. He was a drop-out.

Today, Martin is twenty-eight. He runs a successful business including two mini-super markets and a service station in Lae. He has lots of people working for him. He lives in a big modern house and is well respected in the community.

How could a grade six drop-out become so successful? Read this story and you will learn how he made it to where he is now.

Martin comes from Kalayapu village. It is about fifty kilometres southeast of Nuku station in the Sandaun Province. He went to Windi Community School but he didn't get a place in High School. His mother died when he was a small boy and his father was killed in a car accident four months before Martin completed grade 6. He was left with his sister, who was two years older than him.

One Saturday morning, a PMV was travelling past his village to Nuku station. The PMV had a puncture near Martin's house so they stopped to fix it. Martin was a helpful boy so without being asked, he went to the road and helped the crew to change the tyre. When the new tyre was put on, the driver of the PMV took out a two kina note to give to Martin. However, Martin refused to take the money. The driver then asked Martin, 'Well lad, if you won't take the money, is there something I can do for you?' Martin hesitated so the driver asked again:

'Come on, boy, what do you want?' This time, Martin took a deep breath and replied,

'Can you take me to Wewak, please?' The driver answered,

'Sorry boy, I'm only going as far as Nuku station.'

'Well, take me there then. I want to visit my big sister. She is married to a policeman and they told me to go and see them this week.'

Martin was lying, but he was trying to be as brave as possible. The driver thought for a moment. He had a quick discussion with his crew then said,

'Okay, hop in, we'll take you for free since you helped us.' Martin quickly ran back to his house, grabbed his school certificate in a yellow envelope, plus a few clothes and climbed into the PMV.

Soon his village was out of sight. He stared at the tree tops behind his house as he silently farewelled his village. He was leaving his village for the first time. Instead of going to visit his only sister, he was in fact, leaving her. Suddenly, he felt very sad and scared.

'What am I doing?' he thought to himself. 'I must be crazy!'

The PMV started to speed up once they reached the graded section of the road. But Martin didn't notice the villages they were passing or the other travellers in the PMV. His mind and his concentration were far, far away.

He was still thinking of his Kalayapu village and of his house. He felt sorry for his sister. She was in the gardens when he left, so she wouldn't know where he was.

However, he knew the other boys would tell her what he had done. They'd all seen him jumping on the PMV. He also knew his uncles would look after his sister. That was a good thing about village life. People cared for one another. But he knew his sister would still be very worried. Therefore, he decided to make an effort to send word back to her about his whereabouts once he reached Wewak. Yes, Wewak, that's where he was going, to see his cousin and get a job. He planned to find another PMV at Nuku to take him on to Wewak.

They drove for about three hours before reaching Nuku station at about midday. All the passengers jumped out and Martin followed suit. Then, the driver came out and stared at Martin.

'Kid, are you getting off here or do you want to continue on to Wewak?' Martin didn't answer. He just stood there with his head down. Then, the driver came close, put his right arm on Martin's shoulder and said,

'Now tell me the truth, boy. I'm responsible for bringing you here and I want to be sure that you'll be okay.' Martin looked up into the man's face and started to cry. In a whisper, he told the driver,

'I'm sorry for lying to you. Both my parents are dead. I want to travel to Wewak to stay with my cousin. I want to look for a job. But I don't have any money to pay for my bus fare to Wewak.' The driver replied,

'You'd better not be lying to me again.' Martin crossed his fingers and pointed to the skies, as a sign he was telling the truth. The driver looked into the boy's face and decided to believe him. He put his hand into his front trouser pocket and pulled out some notes, counted them and gave Martin fifteen kina!

'Ten kina is for your bus fare. The rest is for drinks.' Then, as he was turning around to leave he said,

'Bihain yu painim wok stap, yu mas tingim mi. Nem bilong mi em i Tandeka. Mi bilong Marabini.' Tandeka got into his PMV and drove off. What a generous person he was.

Martin could not believe his luck. Maybe his father's spirit was following him around to bring him good luck. A stranger had helped him get to Nuku, and then given him fifteen kina. It was the largest amount of money he had ever held in his hand.

Martin thought back to his father's advice.

'Always be polite and helpful to people, even strangers. If someone helps you when you are in trouble, repay him, if you can. Remember, one good deed deserves another.'

'Yes', he thought to himself, 'that's what I'll do. One day I'll repay Tandeka'. He quickly went into a store nearby, bought a biro and wrote on the envelope containing his certificate,

'Repay Tandeka, Marabini village, fifteen kina plus interest.'

While he was in the store he asked the store keeper where the Wewak bus-stop was.

Martin went to the bus-stop. There were about twelve other people waiting there. No PMV arrived so they just sat and waited patiently. At about two o'clock, an open backed PMV truck arrived. It called for Wewak passengers and soon the PMV was loaded. Martin was one of the first people to jump in. The crew asked for the fares to be paid. Soon, they were driving at top speed towards

Wewak town. Martin felt happy and excited. This was his first trip to Wewak.

After travelling for a while along the bumpy road, Martin started talking to an elderly passenger sitting next to him. He wanted to know all that the old man could tell him about Wewak. How much further was it? How big was it? How many people were there? Were the people friendly?

'Well, my friend, I think we'll get there about midnight. The road is in good condition for once because the grader has been doing its job.' The old man was happy to have someone to talk to, so he told Martin lots of Wewak stories.

They were still driving as it got dark. The PMV was speeding along the coast, following the beach. Eventually, they arrived in Wewak.

Martin was offered a place to sleep in the PMV owner's house. He accepted the offer gladly, because he was too tired to search for his cousin's house.

Next morning he awoke with a scream, after a rat ran over his sleeping body. He said sorry to everyone in the house for disturbing them. Without even having a cup of tea, he asked where the Wewak wharf was, said thanks to the owner of the house, and was off. The wharf was about an hour's walk from the house but he eventually got there.

There were quite a few ships tied up at the wharf. At the entrance gate, a security guard stopped him. Martin told him that he was looking for his cousin, Mainduo Yandanai. The guard went into his small guard-room, flipped through some papers and spoke on his hand-held radio to someone. He then directed Martin to a building saying,

'Your cousin is in the building over there.'

'Thank goodness!' said Martin to himself, feeling very relieved.

Martin moved in with his cousin and began the task of looking for a job. Two months passed. He carried his school certificate around and asked every business in Wewak town for a job, but everywhere he went he got the same answer:

'Sori, no got wok.'

He felt very depressed. He knew he could do a good day's work, so why did everyone say no?

Then one day in May, his luck finally changed. His cousin arrived back at the house in his company vehicle. He opened the door and said,

'Cousin, do you want to work in Port Moresby?' Martin almost fell off the verandah. He could hardly believe his ears. He pinched himself, just to make sure he was awake and not dreaming.

'Yes, please,' was all he could say.

'All right, pack your bags and let's go,' said Mainduo.

It didn't take Martin long to pack, since he only had a few belongings. Within twenty minutes they were at the wharf. His cousin introduced him to the captain of a ship, which was about to depart for Port Moresby.

'Thanks cousin,' he said. 'One day I'll repay you for helping me.'

Before he knew it, they were sailing for Port Moresby. After many days and nights of sailing and stopping, unloading and reloading all sorts of cargo in Madang, Lae, Oro Bay and Alotau, they finally arrived in Port Moresby's Fairfax Harbour.

Martin had quite a shock as he observed the city, as they approached the wharf. He'd never seen so many tall buildings before. He wondered how he was going to cope in such a big city. He thought back to his village, which seemed to be in another world compared to all this.

The captain skillfully manoeuvred the ship alongside the wharf. Soon, they had the gangplank down and people started going ashore while others came aboard. Two Chinese workers came forward and spoke to the captain. Then, they turned to Martin and one of them asked,

'Are you Mainduo's brother?'

'Yes, sir,' replied Martin.

'Okay, come with us.'

Martin had no idea where he was going. He put his trust in the hands of two strangers and off he went.

They got into a small white utility and drove away. They eventually stopped at a place called Boroko. The two men took him into a shop. There, in a small office inside the shop, they introduced him to another Chinese man and then they left.

'You have your school certificate?' asked the man. His name was Mr Fong.

'Yes, sir,' replied Martin, trying to sound as businesslike as possible. Mr Fong studied the certificate, then looked at Martin and said,

'You promise to work hard for me?'

'Yes, sir.'

'Okay, I hope your eyesight is good. I want you to watch everyone who comes into the shop and make sure no one steals anything.'

'Yes, sir,' replied Martin and he walked to the corner. That was his first day at his new job.

During the next five years, Martin learned the whole trade store business from Mr Fong. He learned good manners, how to talk to customers, how to balance the accounts, how to save his own money, how to budget, how to use his time wisely and how to discipline himself.

There were days when Martin didn't feel like getting out of bed, but on those days he forced himself. He knew there were at least twenty other boys hanging around, just

waiting for him to put a foot wrong. He didn't want to lose his job.

Mr Fong taught Martin how to order goods and work out the sale price. He learned how to display goods and how to control the movement of people in and out of the shop. Mr Fong was a good boss to his workers. He was fair but firm. Because Martin was a good worker he was allowed to sleep in a small room at the back of the shop. He acted as security at night.

One Sunday morning, as Martin was returning from church service, he stopped at a street market to buy some *buai*. However, he couldn't afford the expensive prices. He had noticed how prices had gone up in Port Moresby over the last year. The market price was about thirty to forty toea per *buai*. His thoughts returned to his village in Kalayapu. The family had plenty of *buai* trees and in Wewak town you could buy one bundle for just ten toea!

Suddenly, he had an idea. From that day on, his life changed forever. He remembered Mr Fong's advice.

'Always look around you. Where people live, there is always a way to make money. And when you see that opportunity, grab it before someone else does.'

'Yes! That is it!' he thought to himself. '*Buai!* I will order it from Kalayapu and resell it in Port Moresby. My sister can send it to me! I'll benefit and the family back home will benefit.' He felt excited.

He went home and gave the idea more thought. He decided to confide in Mr Fong. Mr Fong could give him some advice on how to order and how much to charge in order to make a profit.

So Martin began his betel nut business and what a business it was! By June 1986, he was the major betel nut wholesaler in the city and business was booming. With a bit of help from Mr Fong, he had no difficulty in getting a loan from the bank.

Soon, he was flying in about one hundred copra bags full of betel nut every week from Wewak. The street vendors bought everything he had, and they still wanted more!

Therefore, he travelled to Madang and the Markham area and arranged for a hundred bags from each place to be sent to Port Moresby. He worked hard to ensure that the quality of betel nut was high, that packaging and transport arrangements were reliable, and that the method of payment was efficient.

By September 1986, Martin was receiving three hundred bags of betel nut per week. The fresh betel nuts were in high demand in the city and selling fast.

He was the only wholesaler in the city supplying the main markets and the street vendors. He advised his buyers to charge a reasonable price to the consumers, so they could sell out quickly but still make a good profit. That is another thing Mr Fong had taught him. He had said,

'If you buy as a wholesaler or retailer, buy plenty. Then, resell at a fair price, but enough to give yourself a small profit. By not being too greedy, you will sell more. And by selling more, you will soon add up all the small profits to give you a bigger profit. However, if you charge high prices, you will only sell a few items. You will chase customers away and make a loss because many of your items will not be bought.'

Mr Fong, as well as being a friend to Martin, was also his business adviser. Although Mr Fong volunteered his advice freely, Martin insisted on paying his friend a consultancy fee, based on how much profit the business was making.

Martin could hardly believe the amount of money his small business brought him. By December 1986, he had fully paid up his bank loan and the interest. Now, he was starting to make big money! He was selling over three hundred bags per week. After subtracting the buying price, transportation costs, advertising costs (on Fong's advice, he advertised his betel nuts in the newspaper), telephone costs and consultation fees, he still made a profit of fifty kina per bag.

By June 1987, Martin had a very healthy bank balance. He bought a house for himself and a second-hand car.

However, there were many others getting into the betel nut business. It wasn't long before there were too many wholesalers and distributors in the city. Martin's sales figures quickly fell from three hundred bags per week to fifty. The fierce competition soon drove some of the wholesalers out of business. Martin's sales eventually increased to about seventy-five bags per week, but he never reached his three hundred mark again.

He was still making good money, but the strong competition continued. Many of the new sellers adopted aggressive business strategies and Martin's sales started falling again. The people who used to do business with him were now buying from their own wantoks. Why should they do business with a stranger when they could do it with their wantoks? In Papua New Guinea, that's a sensible approach and he understood why people did that. He tried to lower his price further, but the wantok connection was too strong. His sales made no improvements. He became very concerned and nervous. He consulted with his old friend, Mr Fong.

Mr Fong's advice was simple.

'First, there was a huge demand for betel nuts in the city. That demand was not met by the local suppliers. Therefore, when you entered the business, you had a big market. The supply was very low, and the demand was very high. Consequently, you had big sales every week and your business expanded very quickly.

'However, today, you have many competitors and as you know, people prefer to do business with their wantoks than with strangers. Therefore, I advise you to close this business. Otherwise, you will lose everything you have made so far. Sell off the remaining stock and then come back and we'll talk some more.'

Martin thanked his friend and left the office. Mr Fong's business advice has always been wise. Martin knew his business success was due partly to the advice Mr Fong had given him.

After Martin had closed down the betel nut business, he and Mr Fong went to the bank for advice. Martin still had a lot of money in his bank account The bank recommended several businesses, some in Lae, others in Moresby. They decided on a service station in Lae.

With help from a bank loan, Martin built a new service station at Top-Town, in Lae. He put the rest of his money in a long-term interest bearing deposit (called an IBD) as a security for his loan.

Martin worked very hard. He made use of all the skills he had learned over the years and he did well, even though running a service station was new to him. He didn't let his lack of education stop him. He was determined to succeed. He maintained close contact with his bank just as Mr Fong had advised him. When they said goodbye at Jackson's airport, Mr Fong said,

'Son, I am so proud of you! You have worked

extremely hard. You have shown a lot of self-discipline and you have succeeded, which makes me very proud of you. I want you to maintain that attitude throughout your business life. If you do that, you will always succeed.

'You haven't let your lack of education stop you. You have taught yourself, which is something to be proud of. Maintain close contact with your bank. They are lending you a lot of money. They will offer you good advice on all business matters, including hiring of staff, staff wage levels, price levels, security, insurance, daily operations, ordering of fuel supplies, methods of payment, etc.

'What you must remember is to learn as much as possible and as fast as you can. Don't be afraid to ask questions when you don't understand. Work hard and I know you'll do well.'

And that was exactly what Martin did. By June 1990, exactly two years after he started his Lae business, he had repaid all his loan, plus the interest. He was now a confident and experienced businessman.

He brought his friend Mr Fong and his cousin Mainduo to Lae, for a holiday. He gave them both a special gift to thank them for all their help.

He also got married to a woman from Lae. She was his company's accountant. And he remembered the man who helped him first all those years ago. He sent a message to Mr Tandeka from Marabini village to travel to Wewak, to collect his paid air ticket and fly to Lae. Tandeka got the message and did as instructed. He was met at Nadzab airport by Martin in his new four wheel drive car. Tandeka, now an old man, could not believe his eyes. Martin bought him a house and gave him a job in the business. Tandeka's fifteen kina was well repaid and with a good interest. Tandeka was very happy.

Martin went home and gave some money to his uncles and to his sister who was now married. Some of his wantoks went to Lae to work for him. Through his hard work and sacrifice, the whole family were benefiting.

Between 1990 and 1995, Martin expanded his business. He bought several mini supermarkets and he now has plans to build a huge supermarket in Top-Town and another in Eriku.

Things to do

1. Write a paragraph to say why Martin succeeded in his business ventures.
2. With a partner, discuss how the two of you could work together to sell something at the market. List the things you would both have to do to make a profit.
3. After leaving school, you decide to live in town. You cannot find a job. In groups, discuss what you could do to help support yourself without resorting to rascal activities.
4. Make a list of what you could do to begin the process of looking for a job.
5. A successful manager must be able to supervise his/her staff. Write a paragraph to say how you would expect your staff to behave if you were a manager and how you would like your manager to treat you.
6. In groups act out a job interview, one person playing the role of the manager, the other playing the role of the person looking for work. Then, reverse your roles.

3 Learning the hard way

Valuka Valuka is a business woman, living in Bialla. She left school at the end of grade 8, and along with most of her friends was called a drop-out.

Valuka is a person who feels satisfied now with her life. She lives in Bialla town with a good husband and three children. She owns two retail shops, one second-hand clothing shop and a new fast-food bar. She also owns two large blocks of oil palm behind her village. Some of these trees are now bearing fruit and are ready for harvesting.

Valuka was not always happy with her life. When she left grade 8, she was angry and frustrated. She wasn't ready to leave school and she felt that the education system was letting her down. It wasn't her fault that there were not enough places for her to go into grade 9.

'I'm not old enough to support myself and help my family,' she thought to herself. 'I'm too young to get married and settle down.'

In fact, she did get married and quickly got herself into all sorts of trouble. You could say that at the end of grade 8 she was still very immature and certainly not ready to commit herself to a lifelong relationship.

When the headmaster of Bialla High School told Valuka that she could not continue onto grade 9, she was shattered. She burst into tears in the office and walked out with her head down. She felt a failure. She went straight to her cubicle in the dorm, lay on her bed and cried uncontrollably throughout that day and on and off, for the next two days.

At the end of the week, she travelled back to her village. It was located only half a kilometre west of Bialla town. She reached her house, sat down under a mango tree and started sobbing again. Her mother came and sat close to her, and put her arm around her daughter.

'What's wrong, little one?' she asked.

'Oh mum, I've failed! I tried so hard, yet they told me I've failed. I'm just a hopeless person and no good to anyone.'

'That's not true, Valuka. If those teachers at the High School say you are a failure, then they don't know what they are talking about.'

Valuka's mother comforted her and assured her that there were many things she could do to make a successful living.

'Never say you are a failure, Valuka. The system has failed you. It's not the other way around. There are too many kids getting thrown out of school at the end of grade 8. They need more teachers and more schools. It's not your fault. We will never blame you. We will stand by and support you all we can, so don't worry. Come, let's go and make some tea.'

Valuka's mum tried to sound cheerful, but deep down she was very worried about her daughter. Valuka was only fourteen years old, but was already a big girl. For those who didn't know her, they would have thought Valuka was sixteen or seventeen years old and this worried Valuka's mother.

Valuka lived with her parents and joined in with village life. She helped her parents in the family's small cocoa plot and in the betel nut gardens. The family were lucky because they had some cash coming in. They had plenty of food from their gardens and caught fish from the sea. Overall, they had a happy village life and had no problems to face, unlike other families living in the urban settlements.

At the end of the year, Valuka did something quite out of character. She went against her parents' wishes and got married. She was just fifteen years old.

Like most kids her age, she was looking for a bit of excitement in her life. She wanted a change. Well, she certainly got one. She married a very handsome, young man who had completed his grade ten education at Kimbe High School. His name was Frank. Frank had a job as a sales clerk in a Bialla wholesale store.

Valuka's parents didn't mind Valuka having Frank as a friend but they were totally against the idea of them getting married. They felt that Valuka and Frank were both too young to handle the pressures and workloads of married life. They even refused to take any bride price in the hope that this would make Valuka change her mind.

Valuka refused to listen to any advice on the matter. She was determined to marry Frank. Frank was a good-looking guy, so she didn't want to lose him to another girl. Also, Frank had a job, was very charming and promised to look after her. Furthermore, Valuka thought such a man would not come into her life again so she decided to marry him. She told herself that her parents and the other elders in the village were just getting worried for nothing.

But this was a terrible mistake. She would soon realise how foolhardy she was.

Only a few months after their marriage, the problems started. Frank was always coming home late from work. He was drinking almost every second day. Soon, there was not enough money to buy even the basics. This led to difficulties with budgeting the family income.

Also, Frank was bringing home many of his young workmates and other drinking mates to their small flat. This put more demands on their food supplies, created a lot of noise for the neighbourhood and privacy was non-existent.

To make matters worse, some of Frank's young buddies were clearly showing more than a friendly interest in Valuka, especially when they had been drinking. This made Frank furious and jealous, and fierce fights usually erupted. Frank always blamed his wife, saying she was being too friendly with his mates.

These problems increased. Valuka was under a lot of pressure and she was not handling the situation well. She was too embarrassed to ask her parents for help. She became worried and highly disillusioned. She considered divorce. She thought of running away to Kimbe and even of committing suicide.

Like all good mothers, Valuka's mother had been monitoring her daughter's behaviour since her marriage. Just when Valuka was about to do something silly, she decided it was time for some straight talking with her daughter.

Valuka broke down and cried. The pressures had been too much for her. She was also very surprised to see how her mother has read all her problems correctly. She started to realise that her mother knew more about life and marriage than she first thought. She realised that she should have taken her mother's advice about the marriage. Then, she would not be in this situation now.

'You have to talk to your husband, Valuka and get him to stop his drinking. It's bad for his body and his spirit and it's bad for the marriage.'

However, the situation did not improve. Frank was not prepared to listen to his wife. He didn't want his friends to think his wife was bossing him about. One evening, Valuka saw Frank with another girl behind the flower gardens at the back of their flat. She lost her mind.

She ran back to the flat, grabbed a long kitchen knife and ran into the garden. She hid behind the tall flowers. They did not see her approach in the dark. When she saw them kissing, she lunged at the girl and stabbed her with the knife!

There was a piercing scream and the girl collapsed. She lost a lot of blood and quickly became unconscious. She did not die, but was severely injured and her right leg was paralysed for life.

Of course, Valuka was arrested and taken to court. Her guilt was obvious to everyone and in spite of her age and previous good record, Valuka was sentenced to jail for two years with hard labour.

She was devastated. If only she had listened to her parents' advice. She couldn't bear to look at her mother's face, as they led her away to jail. She knew her mum had been right when she said the marriage wouldn't work. Why, oh why hadn't she listened? Now, it was too late. She had made a mistake and now she was paying the price. Her marriage was in tatters and her freedom was gone.

Valuka spent two years in Kimbe prison. Her parents visited her whenever they could. They gave her advice and encouraged her to complete her prison term without making trouble with anyone. They tried to give her hope for the future so that she wouldn't feel too depressed or guilty.

Valuka had many terrible experiences in jail. She didn't tell her mother everything, as she knew it would upset her too much. She was assaulted by warders and prisoners. She survived, by dreaming about what she would do on her release. It was a two year nightmare and when she eventually got out, she rarely talked about it with anyone.

Her release from prison came one wonderful Thursday morning in July. Her parents were there to welcome her and take her home. They all cried with joy. She promised her parents she would never disgrace them or herself again.

As soon as they arrived home, Valuka started to tell her parents what she had been planning whilst in jail.

'I want to go into business,' she announced.

Whilst in jail, Valuka had made friends with a woman prisoner who was an accountant. She had been jailed for stealing K15 000 from her employers. After they had become friends, they talked for hours about different ways of earning a living. They decided that a good way would be to sell betel nuts and mutrus in the main centres. Betel nuts and mutrus were plentiful in West New Britain. On the other hand, many centres were in short supply of the stuff. It would be a profitable business to set up, as long as it was well planned.

Her parents decided to give her a chance and lent her K650 from their savings to start the business.

But first, they insisted that Valuka should leave her husband. They all met together with her husband's parents and got an agreement for the customary marriage to end.

As soon as the split-up was out of the way, Valuka began her business with help from the wantoks in Lae and

Port Moresby. It was a bold plan by a girl who had faced many problems, but who had learned many lessons.

The Lae operation was very successful. From the K650 investment, they made a profit of K3850.

The Moresby operation was also a success.

Valuka soon had a large bank balance.

She decided it was time to expand the business and direct her attention to other business opportunities. With the help of a bank loan, she bought a second-hand clothing business in Bialla, from a family who were leaving the area.

The branch manager at the bank gave her lots of advice on the purchase and continued to support her whenever she felt she needed help. He became a good friend.

She found this business both challenging and rewarding. It was rewarding because she was making a good living in her own place. The increase in the number of oil palm blocks and the logging operations in the Bialla area, meant there was more money coming to the people. People were buying clothes and food from her shop.

It was challenging because she was learning new business skills and using problem-solving techniques. The branch manager from the bank continued to advise her.

Two years later, Valuka bought another shop.

She also got married. She married the man from the bank. Valuka's parents were delighted. Valuka's husband resigned from the bank to help Valuka manage the expanding business. Soon they bought another retail shop.

In 1991, they planted two big blocks of oil palm on Valuka's land. Valuka used the business assets as security for a bank loan.

Today, Valuka is a very confident person with good

business skills and an optimistic and mature outlook on life. She also has three children.

She plans to develop her land by planting more oil palm trees on both her land and her clan's land. She believes the Bialla area can become rich with oil palm. She also wants to help create employment opportunities for her people.

She is heavily involved in community affairs and is regarded as a leader in the area. She is also a member of the governing body for several schools. Valuka often gives talks to schools and youth groups.

What has made Valuka so successful? She cites the problems of her first marriage, her prison experience and her divorce. These problems, she says, have taught her some very tough lessons.

'If you encounter problems in life, you must learn from the experience. Look for the positive side. It's easy to blame others and feel sorry for yourself. Something good can always come from a bad experience, if you make an effort to set a new course for yourself. Also, be a good listener. Never think you know it all. Don't close your mind. Continue to learn.'

She strongly believes that the future for Papua New Guinea is based on the land.

'You can use the land to improve your living standards,' she says. 'Look around you. You have kunai grass, vines, trees, creeks, sand, stones and rocks, water, minerals, peanuts, sugarcane, mangoes, pitpit, etc. All these things have a use. Do your feasibility studies and develop these things into marketable products.'

Valuka warns young people not to dream about finding employment in offices and factories in the towns.

'These are false and dangerous expectations. Such

expectations are already causing disillusionment and frustration within our society.

'Towns and cities don't have enough gardens, fresh creeks, rivers, trees, firewood, birds and wildlife. People living in the towns don't have many of their cousins, uncles, clan members or wantoks to give them support.

'Towns are full of strangers, both nationals and foreigners, who don't care for the welfare of others. It is a place of cars, buildings, dust, hold-ups, police raids and prison cells. It is a tough environment,' she warns.

She recommends village life to a troublesome urban life. She feels strongly that Papua New Guineans can use the village environment to have a satisfying and fulfilling life.

'By remaining in the village, you avoid many problems that are found in towns and cities. You will not lose your land. Your children will not be dislocated from village life and roam the streets like lost people in a strange land.

'I want my children and grandchildren to live in the village. If they go for studies and further training, then I want them to come back to the village and put their skills to good use. I want my children to know their culture and their identity and feel proud of their history. I don't want them roaming the streets like lost dogs. This is Papua New Guinea. It is a Melanesian tradition. You must always love your village, its people and its surroundings. You must live your life within your society.

'When you die in a village, the whole village will attend your funeral, cry for you, and mourn your passing.

'In the towns and cities, only the ambulance driver and the priest will be there to receive your coffin! The whole world will not give a damn about your death!'

So where would you choose to live?

Things to do

1 Imagine you are in prison. Write a short story about your experiences. If possible, before you start your story, interview someone who has been to prison or who has worked in a prison.

2 Discuss the following questions in your groups.

What is a good age to get married?

What things do you look for when choosing a marriage partner?

For how long should you know someone, before getting married to them?

3 Valuka identified the betel nut as a marketable item, growing in abundance in her area. She sold the betel nut to markets in Lae and Port Moresby where the demand for betel nuts was high. Identify things in your area that could be sold both locally and further afield, so that you could make a living from the sale of the goods. Discuss your answers in class. Tell the class what, why, when and how you could make a living.

4 The long journey

This is a story about a village boy's determination to get a good education and a job. Kelea Ponduai is now a chief inspector with the police. He is about thirty years old and married with two children. He comes from Uro village, in the last Wiru area of Pangia district, in the Southern Highlands Province.

Ponduai's story is interesting for many reasons. He was the first boy from his area to go to a High School. He had to attend a high school in another district, some sixty kilometres away from his village. The school he attended had no boarding facilities. It was very difficult for him to stay at school. But he never gave up and he went on to be the first person in his district to become a police officer.

Ponduai is not sure what year he was born because his parents did not keep a record. They had never been to school.

Ponduai grew up in the village, surrounded by rainforests and creeks. He had a wonderful childhood. When he was very young, his mother would carry him around with her. He would sit on top of the bilum on his mother's back and observe the world, while she walked to the gardens to work, or feed the pigs, or carry water back to the village. When he wanted milk, his mother would feed him. If he was hungry, mother would give him mashed banana or soft kaukau. During the many trips to the gardens, mother would always carry him because he was too small to walk.

It often rained. The tracks went over hills and into valleys and were muddy and overgrown by bush. Not many people used the tracks. The population of the area was small.

Ponduai had no clothes, no bilums, no tangets. When it rained, he was put in a bilum and carried with a pandanus umbrella over him. He was dry and comfortable inside and would mumble away to himself. His mother did the hard work of carrying him on top of a bag of kaukau and greens, as well as having a bundle of firewood on her head. She would use a walking stick to support herself. During the night, he would always sleep close to his mother's belly. If he wanted milk at night, it was always available.

When he was about five years old, he started to leave his mother. During the day, he sometimes stayed back to play with the other kids. There were about five or six of them. They would roam around the village looking for things to do. If somebody suggested a game, they would all join in. A favourite daily pastime was story-telling. They told exciting stories about killing pigs and distributing their parts. They would draw pictures on the ground. Other favourite stories included searching for mushrooms in the forest, searching for frogs, hunting trips or gardening adventures.

When they got tired of telling stories, they would walk down to the creek for water. Sometimes, they spent the whole afternoon playing in the mud. By sunset, they all slowly disappeared to their houses, hoping to find some food to eat. Often they would still be covered in mud and their parents had to send them back to the creek for another wash! If the parents did not come home quickly, they would go to the village boundary fence, and sit and wait. They all enjoyed the sight of their mothers returning from the gardens.

When Ponduai was about seven years old, he stayed only with the other boys. He avoided the girls! Sometimes, the boys would make bows and arrows and spears. When they went to the gardens they planted sugarcane or bananas. Kaukau and other vegetables were left to the girls to plant.

Sometimes all the boys would stay back in the village while everyone else went to their gardens. The boys would get their bows and arrows and decide where to go and hunt for birds. The older boys usually decided and the younger boys like Ponduai just followed.

When they left the village fence, they liked to sing on their way to the hunting ground. The older boys would go first and try to identify the birds, that were eating or napping in the trees.

When they got to the bush they generally moved in complete silence, in single file or in two lines, about a hundred metres apart. Even the breaking of dead branches or coughing was forbidden. Talking had to be in whispers or by using hand signals and facial signs.

Every hundred metres or so, the leaders would stop, listen and then imitate bird songs. If the birds replied, they would follow the direction of the birds' songs. Sometimes, they were lucky but at other times, they were not. If they were lucky enough to shoot some birds with their bows and arrows, they would take them to the river, make a fire and roast them. They would all share the meat between them.

They would then remove their bilums, cover themselves with some leaves and swim in the river. If they caught some fish, they would cook it over the fire and of course, share it amongst themselves. If some boys had gardens nearby they would go and collect pitpit, corn or sugarcane. Digging of kaukau was not allowed, as it was women's food. They only harvested men's food. They would tell stories, laugh, play some boy-games and swim in the river again. Life was great fun!

Normally, it was easy to locate the group by the river because they were so noisy. Other boys who had gone out with their fathers early in the morning would now desert their fathers and join the group. The boy-games, story telling and swimming would continue until late afternoon. Then, the older boys would decide it was time to go home. They would cut some firewood, share the load between them and carry it home. They normally sang most of the way because that was the way men moved around. Likewise, the girls would follow a different track to the village and sing girl-songs.

Sometimes, the boys would also accompany their fathers and uncles and help them do the work reserved for men. They helped to clear the bush to make new gardens, fix garden fences, make traps for wild pigs and cuscus, check sugarcane and banana plants, or clear bushes around the pandanus trees.

This was Ponduai's world. He and the other boys had heard stories about strangers bringing new trade goods to the area, but their lives had not been affected by these changes. Ponduai and his friends had never seen the strangers. His people were already using knives and axes but there were no spades or modern-day clothes in the village.

One day, it was announced that a stranger was coming to the village. When the stranger arrived, Ponduai and the other boys ran into the bush. They were scared. A few days later, they heard a plane flying overhead. They could not see it because it was above the clouds. The elders said, since it was flying high in the sky, it must be a *patere balus* (Catholic church plane) and not a *missin balus* (Lutheran church plane). The general belief was that the *patere balus* was better and smarter than the *missin balus*.

A few days later, the villagers started building a road. This was the first sign of real change in the village. The road eventually connected all the villages in the area together. The villagers worked on the roads from Monday to Friday, from early morning to midday. The local headman became the *bos boi* and later was made the councillor. Within three months, the road to Pangia station was complete. Life changed forever for the people.

When Ponduai was about eight years old his life took a step in a new direction. His uncle told him to get ready to go to school at a place called Windi, some ten kilometres from the village. The bush had been cleared and many kunai houses built. The councillor had announced that this *skul*, was where the young children learn the *pasin bilong white man na kisim save.* Ponduai was taken to the school for registration. A white man told Ponduai to put his right arm over his head and touch his left ear. This was the way their ages were judged! Those who could not touch the left ear were allowed to attend school. Those who could, were told to go home because they were too old. So began Ponduai's school life.

Ponduai was a small boy compared to the other boys at the school. But he tried hard. He was a bright student and interested in his work. He listened carefully to his teachers and followed their instructions, as well as listening to his parents and others in the village. He was learning about two worlds. The world at home and the world outside.

Getting to school each day was difficult. For six years Ponduai walked ten kilometres to school and ten kilometres home. He had to cross two small rivers, three mountains and two swampy areas. When it rained heavily, he was cut off by the rivers or the flooded swamps. Sometimes he was late for school. His teacher would call him up to the front of the class and ask why he was late. His answers were never accepted. He was usually caned four or five times on the buttocks. On the first swing, he would start crying. But the teacher never showed any mercy for a crying student.

The six years seemed to last forever. Then in November 1975, two months after the Independence celebrations (something he never understood as a small boy), his community school life came to an end. He completed grade six. And Ponduai came second in a class of 56! During a big gathering where parents and friends from all the villages were assembled, it was announced that Ponduai had won a place at Ialibu High School. The school was in Ialibu district, about sixty kilometres from Uro village. Ponduai left the community school for the last time, feeling sad but also happy and excited.

Going to High School was a big event. Ponduai was the first boy from his village to go to High School. It was talked about often in the village, over the Christmas holidays.

In January 1976, his father bought him two pairs of shorts, two short-sleeved shirts, one jumper and a towel. That was to last him for the next four years. He got rid of his *ass-tanget* and wore the new clothes. He looked different and felt different. He was the only boy in the village with shorts and he felt a bit embarrassed.

At last the big day arrived and Ponduai left for Ialibu High School. It was his first time to leave the area. He was accompanied by his father and also boys from other nearby villages who had also been selected to go to High School. They walked to Pangia station first. It was Ponduai's first time to see the station and hear the generator's engine, and see such things as the horses; the white people; the tractor; the *haus kapa*; the airstrip; the stores filled with colourful goods; the well-dressed storekeepers with biros stuck in their hair; policemen; warders and their *ol karabus*; a bridge across the river; to name just a few. He was amazed and confused.

After resting for about an hour at Pangia, they continued on with their journey. Their destination was Ialibu. They followed the Ialibu-Pangia road. A few tractors and trucks passed them but they were not picked up. They walked and they walked, until they reached Ialibu station. The sun was already going over the mountains. They had walked more than sixty kilometres!

Ialibu station was much bigger than Pangia. There was a larger population, bigger roads and a lot more traffic. The town's roads were laid with white *karanas* and were much smoother than the Pangia road that was made from huge river stones making walking painful and difficult.

Ialibu had sporting facilities for basketball, soccer and rugby league. Ponduai had never seen a rugby field or watched a game of rugby. Some expatriates were playing on a white sandy patch with a net across it, hitting small green balls back and forth. It looked uninteresting to Ponduai. He wondered what that game was called.

At last they arrived at the High School for their first night in a very cold climate.

Ponduai's father left the next day after paying K125 for school fees. He gave Ponduai a hug and said,

'Well, man, I'm leaving you now.' He spoke first in the Wiru language and then in Tok Pisin he said:

'Yu mas skul gut. Mi no laik harim kainkain stori. Tingting bilong yu mas stap long skul tasol. Na lukautim yu yet.' He moved forward to hug Ponduai again and before Ponduai could say anything, his dad was already walking away. Ponduai just stood there, his eyes filled with tears and his head full of questions.

'What will I do now? Who will look after me here? Will the older students fight me?'

Within a few days, school started and Ponduai was too busy to worry about loneliness, his parents or his village.

But life in High School soon became very tough. Ponduai coped well with his school work. However, he had no proper place to live. The school was a day school and had no boarding facilities. His village was far, far away.

He had to live in an open *kunai* house built for Pangia students by the Pangia local government council. There was nothing inside the house. Their beds were mats made from kunai leaves and spread on the ground. They had to dig their own toilets near the house. As for drinking and washing water, they dug small pits in the nearby swamp. They had to buy and cook their own food

A lot of the Pangia students went without lunch. A few who had extra money would buy biscuits in the nearby trade stores. When it rained heavily, the swamp was filled with water. Since their house was built on the swampland, the floor of the house was often waterlogged. The boys could not sleep. Instead, they stayed awake and told stories and played jokes by splashing water on anyone who tried to sleep! Sometimes the jokes turned into fights because the splashing made someone's blanket really wet.

Other times, it became funny because some tried to escape the water by climbing up towards the roof and sleeping on the platform that supported the roof. When other students found out, they were dragged down or else water was thrown at them to force them down! This was done to stop some boys from finding a good place to sleep whilst others were suffering. To make it worse, all this was happening in pitch darkness, therefore it was both funny and quite dangerous.

Ponduai did not return home until the first term holidays. During term one, Ponduai managed to survive on the K20 that his dad had given him.

Every Saturday morning, he bought a bag of kaukau at Ialibu market. He usually had to pay K1.00. Sometimes he would wait till two or three o'clock when the women started to put more kaukau in each heap. If he was lucky, he could sometimes fill his bag with just fifty or sixty toea. Then, he used the change to buy soap, sugarcane, vegetables or a small tin of fish. He would live on that bag of kaukau until the following Saturday. This budgeting of money continued until the first term break. The main type of food Ponduai had was kaukau.

However, after the first term break, life became even more difficult. Ponduai's family had no money to give him. His father had to save up for the next year's school fees. At the moment, his father had no coffee. He had planted peanuts but the new plots were not ready. Ponduai's father told him,

'Son, I am really sorry for you. You are a still a small boy. You are not really grown up like the other students. The High School is too far away for you to return each weekend to get your food. Someone could kill you on the long road, or, you could get lost and die of hunger. Therefore, if you want to leave school, that is all right with me.'

Ponduai burst into tears. He could see the pain in his father's eyes and he felt so sorry for him and his mother. He knew the family was poor, and that his father could not support him financially. Ponduai felt terrible. He didn't know what to do. How could he walk back to his village for food every weekend? His father had nobody else in the family who had extra money to spare. What could he do?

Tears were still rolling down his cheeks as he stood up, picked up his kaukau that was packed in a rice bag and balanced it on his shoulders. Then, he started walking. He didn't say anything. His father didn't say a word either. Ponduai just kept walking, with the tears still rolling down his face. He was going back to school! He would try! He was not going to give up.

For the next three and a half years, Ponduai followed a set routine. He would return home every Friday afternoon with some of the other Pangia students. They walked slowly along the Pangia-Ialibu road. They would walk the whole night! Many students hurt their feet because they had no shoes. By 5.00 a.m. on Saturday they arrived at Pangia market.

From Pangia, Ponduai walked on until he reached his village. He stayed in the village for Saturday night and then began his return journey the next morning. He walked with his bag of kaukau balanced on his shoulder. He met the other boys at Pangia station and they began the long walk back to Ialibu. It was so tiring. By the time they reached the school, it was about eleven o'clock at night or even later.

The boys would simply drop all their bags, fall onto their kunai grass mats and fall asleep, hungry, cold and totally exhausted.

Because of the hard life, many Pangia students failed their grade 8 examinations. Out of the fourteen Tunda community school students that had started grade 7, only two remained to go onto grades 9 and 10. Ponduai was one of them.

Life continued to be a struggle for him. He had no wantoks in Ialibu to help him. Occasionally, he did not go back to the village for the weekend because his mother was able to give him a bit of money to buy food. However, most of the time, he continued walking back and forth. On many occasions, he felt like giving up. Many times, he walked back and forth, alone. Sometimes he was afraid of bad spirits. Other times, he was afraid of the people he met on the road. On many occasions, after walking with his bag of kaukau in the hot sun or heavy rain, he would stop to take a break. Without even realising, he had tears cascading down his face. Why was life so difficult? Was it worth it? Why was he going through this for four years?

It was the advice from his headmaster, a man from Israel that helped to keep him going. The headmaster had said,

'Son, I know your village is far away. I know you have no friends around here. I know you are walking home to collect food every weekend and that is a very hard challenge. But you have won the challenge. That shows you are strong, both mentally and physically. Therefore, you must not give up now. You have only six months left. You must complete your schooling. You must push on. You must graduate.'

And so Ponduai pushed on for the remaining six

months. His high school years came to an end and with it, all the hardships he had suffered over the four years. Ponduai was the happiest student in the school after his final grade 10 examinations. He had concentrated and studied hard and achieved an excellent result. He received credits and above, in all his subjects, and was accepted at Sogeri National High School.

After two years at Sogeri, where he did well again in all his subjects, he was accepted as a police cadet at Bomana Police College. After two years training, he graduated as the top student in his class.

He has been in the police force for the last twelve years. He is now a chief inspector and helps to train other police officers. He is married with two children.

Ponduai has attended many overseas courses in Australia, Great Britain, New Zealand and Singapore. He is very happy with his pay, work conditions and his job. When Ponduai thinks back to those very difficult years, he is very happy that he never gave up, despite all the great hardships that he had to endure. His advice to young students is this:

'Concentrate on your school work and study hard. Listen to your parents and teachers. And above all, do not give up, when the going gets tough. Keep pushing on. You will win!'

Things to do

1 Research the traditional culture and way of life of your people before Europeans came into contact with them.

2 Research and write a short account of the first recorded contact between Europeans and your people.

5 Working in paradise

Misima Island is located on the far eastern fringes of Papua New Guinea. It has a population of about 21 000 people.

Today, the island's economy is largely based on the large Misima gold mine. The mine is situated on the southern coast of the island. Bwagoia town, the government administrative centre is some seven kilometres east of the mine site. Most mine workers live close to Bwagoia.

Misima islanders make their living by working at the mine, selling fish and sea produce at Bwagoia town market. They also sell fresh vegetables to other local people, to the government workers and to the mine employees.

The beauty of Misima island is well known. It is a perfect tourist resort island that is yet to be developed. The people are very friendly. The island is almost crime and trouble free. It has a good airport. It has beautiful, white sandy beaches all around the island. It has diving potential. The crystal clear creeks and the tropical rainforest make it a perfect environment for ecotourism.

This story is about a woman who promotes tourism on Misima. She owns and operates a small guest-house on the eastern fringes of Bwagoia town. She has been operating this business for five years. Recently, she has expanded her services to include diving tours.

This is her account of how she started her business in 1991.

Betty completed High School in 1985. She gained good grades in the core subjects and was offered a place at Popondetta School of Nursing. However, she declined the offer because she wanted to get married.

In December 1985, she married an Australian mine worker at Misima. He was a bit older than her, but was a good husband and took good care of her. Betty's attempts to get a job at the mine were unsuccessful.

The couple had their first child in January 1987, a girl. The next year, the husband's parents visited them from Brisbane, to see the new child. They stayed in Misima for two weeks.

One day, during their stay, Betty's in-laws started telling her about their own suburb not far from Brisbane. It was a major tourist centre that attracted many tourists because of its wonderful climate and clean, scenic beaches.

The old couple then talked about their impressions of Misima. They said Misima Island was very beautiful. It had all the features that could make it a major tourist resort for Papua New Guinea.

'Why don't you and Neil think about setting up a tourist business,' the old man said.

That evening, when Neil returned home from work, the idea was discussed further. Neil, an engineer by profession, quickly realised that his parent's idea was worth further research.

They agreed to do a feasibility study regarding the prospect of commencing tourism operations on Misima. From the findings of that study, they would determine whether any profitable business opportunity in tourism existed on the island, and also to what extent the business could develop. Only then, would they decide whether or not to go ahead with the idea.

Neil's mum and dad, offered to do the survey. Neither of them had any training or professional knowledge in the tourism industry, but because they lived in an area that actively promoted tourism, they had some idea of the things that were needed.

They all sat down together and discussed what they should look for in their feasibility study. The next day, the old couple worked on the plan. By eight o'clock that evening, the outline for the feasibility study was completed. The next day, they were ready to start their survey.

Within seven days the feasibility study report was completed. The couple had looked at such things as: the number of small, nearby islands that could hold a guest house, hotel or major resort; other suitable spots along the coast or inland; the views of landowners in these areas towards tourism; the number of flights into Misima; the number of visiting tourists and other people arriving in Misima over the seven day period by both air and sea; the number of ships calling into Misima each week; the island's law and order situation; the views of local elders, church leaders, politicians, businessmen and others regarding tourism on Misima; the PMV system; the transport system provided by small dinghies; the availability of local artefacts; the wealth of local traditions and cultures; the beauty of the islands; the presence of tropical rainforest and wildlife; and the availability of good safe diving spots.

The report concluded by saying, Misima had a huge potential. It went further and recommended that, Betty and Neil should attempt tourism development on Misima by starting with a small guest-house. They recommended the guest-house should be located close to

Bwagoia town, along a hill that overlooks a beautiful stretch of white beach, with a crystal clear river and a creek running on either side of the beach. In front of the beach there were three beautiful small islands that had good diving spots nearby. Behind the hill was an undisturbed typical Papua New Guinea rainforest. The location was perfect for a tourism business.

After presenting the report, discussing it in detail and giving some advice to Betty and Neil, the old couple left for Australia. They'd had a wonderful holiday in a place they considered to be paradise. They wished Neil and Betty good luck and promised to keep in touch regarding the new project.

Betty and Neil discussed the feasibility report again between themselves. In their discussions, they tried to answer some of their concerns. Could they succeed? Did they have the skills and knowledge to run a guest house? Did they have enough money to start the business? If not, where would they borrow from and how much should they borrow? What were the licence fees? Who gave approval to start this sort of business?

By the end of the week, they'd made their decision to give it a go. They would build a guest house on Misima.

But like any major operation, they had to come up with an outline action plan. This is what their plan looked like in July 1988.

<u>Aug 88-Dec 90</u>: Guest-house/Hotel Management course for Betty through a correspondence school in Melbourne. Cost of the diploma course K3000.

<u>Jan 89-June 89</u>: Detailed feasibility study by a wantok of Betty's who was an accountant. This study would form the basis for a bank loan application.

July 89: If the feasibility study was positive they would submit a proper loan application to the bank for a twenty room guest-house.
Dec 89: If the bank loan failed, they would borrow money from Neil's parents to start the business, together with their savings. They had some money in Neil's saving account, but not enough. Based on the feasibility study, the total amount of capital initially required to start the guest-house and operate it was K30 000.
Jan 90-Dec 90: Betty would complete her Diploma correspondence course. Meanwhile, the family would prepare for start up by: registering a company; leasing/renting local land; finalising arrangements with landowners; finding a small contractor to plan and build the guest house; interviewing possible staff; talking to insurance firms; getting advice from the tourism promotion authority; planning advertising strategies, e.g. through newspapers, travel magazines, tour promoters in Papua New Guinea and overseas, parents in Australia; and getting assistance from provincial and national Tourism boards where possible.
Sept 90-Mar 91: Construction of the guest-house.
April 91: Operations begin.

With the above outline plan, the couple wrote to many correspondence schools to find one that offered a course to suit Betty's needs. In August, Betty was registered and received her first printed study material and so began her Diploma course in guest-house management. She would finish her course in December 1990.

Between August 1988 and December 1990, the couple tried to follow their outline action plan. Some things worked out exactly as planned but others did not and changes had to be made.

Also, throughout the two years before the business opened, the couple learned many things about guest-house management, the tourism industry, and general business practices.

Betty found the course interesting and challenging. With her husband's help, she prepared a course study program that she strictly followed. She encountered problems but with a bit of assistance from Neil she managed to complete the course. Generally, she found the course material well written and easy to follow.

Her husband's understanding, encouragement and support were enormous. Also, she was motivated and committed to completing the course. Other key factors that contributed towards her finishing the course included: her in-laws' and her own parents' support; the prospect of a Diploma qualification; the prospect of owning and managing a guest-house; support from her younger sister in helping with child minding duties.

Throughout the two years preparation period, Betty increased her knowledge in guest-house management and tourism.

They were successful in obtaining the bank loan. Moreover, Betty proudly received her Diploma in December 1990.

Neil's parents helped significantly. Between January and March 1991, Betty went to Australia. Neil's parents secured a three months trainee manager position for Betty in Brisbane and on the Gold Coast. She spent one and half months in a small guest-house on the outskirts of Brisbane and a further one and half months in a small hotel on the Gold Coast. She practised what she had learned on the course. She also picked up lots of new tips due to exposure in a real working environment.

With this additional knowledge, and new found skills and confidence, Betty returned to Misima in early April.

When she arrived back, the guest house was completed, licensed and ready to open. She recruited her staff and gave them two weeks basic training, (to be followed by on-the-job training).

She prepared shift rosters, rules for workers, standards of dress and behaviour of staff, and so on.

They were now truly set to make their dream come true. At last, after two full years of thinking, planning, feasibility studies, courses, and building, their guest-house was ready for business.

It was officially opened on the 2 May 1991. Their very first guests were five American research students who came to stay for two months to research the Misima mine and its effects on the Misima people.

Things to do

1 In groups, plan a small business venture that you want to do. Conduct a feasibility study similar to the one done by Betty and her in-laws. Record your results. State your conclusions.

2 'Ambitious people tend to be successful.' Do you agree or disagree with this statement. Discuss in groups.

3 List five key things you think you need in order to be successful in life.

4 Find out about correspondence courses available to students in Papua New Guinea.

5 Make a list of publications that could help you plan a small business venture. Go to the library, check the newspapers, write to organisations and business houses etc.

6 At the crossroads

My name is John Atara. I'm twenty years old. I come from Barenta village, near Popondetta in the Oro Province. I am the third born in a family of five children. I have three sisters and one brother. My mum and dad live in the village, which is close to town. My dad works as a mechanic with the Works Department in Popondetta.

I went to Daru community school in Daru from 1984 to 1989. When my family moved from Daru back to Popondetta at the end of 1989, I went to Popondetta High School. After grade 10, I entered Goroka Technical College, where I was accepted as an apprentice in a painting and sign-writing course. I completed my one year certificate course in November 1994. I have to say I didn't work very hard while at the college.

Currently, I live in Lae. I've applied for lots of jobs since completing my course at Goroka Technical College but I have not received any job offers so far. And I'm not very confident of receiving offers because I didn't get good results at the college. My high school grades weren't any better.

Right now, I've got lots of worries. I don't know what I'll do if I don't get a job offer. I don't want to go home and face my parents and the others back in the village. I feel ashamed of myself and I don't want my parents to think I'm a failure. I know they'll talk about me behind my back and I couldn't take that. I know it was a struggle for them to keep me at school and I feel I've let them down. They won't have any respect for me. I just can't face going home feeling like this.

Maybe I'll stay with the wantoks for a while in Lae and then move on to Port Moresby. But what can I do in these cities?

I can't expect the wantoks to look after me properly. They've all got their own kids and nobody has much money to spare. I'm sure they won't want me around for too long. Who's going to buy my food, clothes and give me bus fares? What can I do? Just sit around in town? Maybe I'll join one of the gangs that some of the city boys are in.

These questions are going through John's mind as he sits in the Lae botanical gardens. People are busy walking up to top town or down to Eriku. Nobody stops to ask him about his worries. He just sits on a bench and stares up into the tall trees. A magnificent bird of paradise sings loudly in the tree above, then, suddenly, cuts off singing and flies across to another tree. It flies directly over John's head, and as John looks up, deposits a lump of warm stuff right on his face. He knows at once what it is. Even the birds are against him today. Angrily, John walks to the creek nearby and washes his face.

John walks down to Eriku, with one hand in the back pocket of his blue jeans. He keeps his head down, as worried people often do and he walks very slowly. His thoughts turn inwards again. He feels sorry for himself. Why has he ended up like this? Will things work out for him later? He can't find the answers to these questions.

At Eriku, he stops at the bus stop by the oval and sits on the bench. The place is full of hustle and bustle, as people come and go, laughing and joking. He can hear many languages that he doesn't understand. He guesses there are about a hundred people at the bus stop. Lots of people all talking in their own tok ples, including a few, talking in English and Tok Pisin. He thinks to himself, 'All these people have a purpose to their lives and look at me. Mr Nobody with nowhere to go and nothing to do. Why am I the odd one out?'

The people at the bus stop come from all over Papua New Guinea. Some are Tolai, some women are from North Solomons, some are Simbus, some are Sepiks, some are Keremas and others are from Mendi, Wabag, Manus, Kimbe, Samarai and Daru.

Although, he is in the middle of a big crowd, he feels very much alone. Nobody has recognised him, said hello to him, offered him a smoke or some *buai*. Nobody has looked at him, and asked him why he feels so unhappy. This is so different from his home life. Many people would have recognised him, greeted him and offered him a smoke or *buai*. They would have shown that they cared for him.

Suddenly, there is a lot of noise from behind him, under the big rain trees. A blue police van has just pulled up and some policemen step out from the car. One of them has a rifle that is pointing upwards to the sky. John gets scared at the sight of the policemen and the rifle. Then, the policemen walk around and collect all the betel nut from the women vendors.

John feels angry. Why are the police doing this? These women are trying to make a living while providing a service to the travelling public. As the cops drive off, he thinks what an upside down world it is. He cannot understand why the grassroots, who are trying to help themselves and earn a bit of money, are threatened with rifles by people who are supposed to protect them. Firearms should only be used as a last resort and certainly not against Papua New Guinea mothers selling *buai!*

John went back to the bench. Many PMVs came in and stopped. The boss-crew screamed out: 'Unitech' or '1,2,3,4,5 mile' or 'Kamkum-Unitech' or 'Bundi compound'. The noise from all the screaming boss-crews, sounded like a gaggle of geese! The noise went on non-stop as buses came and went. John still remained in his seat, not knowing exactly what he should do next.

His mind wandered off again to those same questions that were always with him every morning, when he woke up from sleep.

What was he doing in Lae? Should he go home? What would he do? Should he hunt for a job? Would he be successful? He knew his grades were not good enough. Companies always wanted students with good grades. Why didn't he study hard? Why did he waste so much time sitting around with his friends, teasing girls and telling stories? None of those boys or girls were there to help him now. Why did he laugh at all those students who were always in the classroom studying? They all gained good grades and now most were employed or in higher institutions. Why did he make those stupid mistakes? Why didn't the teachers, his friends or his parents warn him about all this? Nobody really warned him that it was going to be this hard. At least his parents should have warned him. Did they want to see him like this? He was so angry with himself. He was also angry with everyone else. Why didn't they prepare him better for life after school?

He felt so hopeless, he was close to tears. But he realised that he was in the middle of a crowd. He got up and walked away. His mind was still looking for answers to these questions. Then, his thoughts went home, to Popondetta and to his village and to his house and to his family. Yes, that was it! It was his parents. He had not studied well because of his parents. They were always arguing and fighting and screaming. Household items, clothes, pots, plates, spoons and cups were always thrown around and damaged. The walls of the house had many battle scars. There was always a fight in the house.

This had worried John as he was growing up. He could not concentrate in class. His mind was usually somewhere else. His parents problem was always troubling him. Why were they always fighting? There was no peace at home. John was not happy at home. He was ashamed of his parents when his friends asked why they were always fighting. He could never read or do his assignments at home. How could you study in that situation? When John tried to, his father never seemed to be interested. He never asked how John was doing in school. John never tried to explain some of his study problems to his parents.

But why didn't he tell his parents that he was getting worried about their fighting? Did his parents know that he was affected? That his schooling was seriously affected? Perhaps this was one reason why he did so badly at school. Maybe he should have talked to them. If they had understood how he felt, perhaps they would have behaved differently. Maybe his parents thought their problems did not affect him. Every time his mother asked how he was, he would answer: 'I'm fine mum.'

'Is your schooling all right?'

'Yes mum.' But he knew, he was lying. If only he had told them the truth. But he couldn't. He was ashamed. He knew he was doing badly, yet he couldn't do anything about it, or so he thought. How could his parents spend time with him if they were fighting all the time? They were carried away with their own problems. He thought his school work really did not matter to them.

John arrived at his wantok's house in the Papuan compound. The house was locked. Everybody must have gone out somewhere. He went under the mango tree and sat down on the grass, he took off his shirt and his shoes. The shade brought coolness to his body. He stretched out on the cool grass. He could smell the freshness of the green leaves. Within a few minutes he was fast asleep. He was hungry and his mind was already confused, after all the heavy thinking. He needed rest and he went into a deep sleep, hoping that when he woke up those questions would be gone from his mind.

Things to Do

1 What are the main reasons for John's poor grades at school.

2 Write a paragraph to say what John might have done to solve some of his problems while at school.

3 What do you think the school could have done to help John perform better.

4 In groups act out what John and his parents could have done to help solve his problems at school.

5 Make a list of the things that stop you from studying.

6 Decide how you can try to solve these problems:
- by yourself
- with your teachers
- with your parents
- with your chaplain
- with your friends
- with your wantoks

7 John is now, 'at the crossroads'. Make a list of the things John can do to help himself.

Printed in Australia
19 Oct 2018
687755